PRAISE FOR *MAPS AND TAPES*

"A nostalgic revisiting of Adrienne Robillard's life as a female musician, captured in tender vignettes."

—Lisa Nola
creator of the *Listography Journal* series

"Some people dream of joining a band, but Adrienne Robillard shows how it's done. In her gripping memoir, she goes from the new girl at school to a founding member of an indie band that eventually brings her to the UK and Europe. *Maps and Tapes* is for anyone who has ever wanted to follow a dream and not had the encouragement to try."

—Susan Blumberg-Kason
author of *Good Chinese Wife*

"*Maps and Tapes* is a beautifully rendered, gorgeously grounded and poignantly nostalgic story of a girl's coming of age in music. Robillard moves us across space and time, and her prose—like the music nestled within it—perfectly captures the thrills and longings of an era."

—Liz Harmer
author of *The Amateurs* and *Strange Loops*

Maps and Tapes

THE HALIʻA ALOHA SERIES

Maps and Tapes

ADRIENNE ROBILLARD

LEGACY ISLE
PUBLISHING

THE HALI‘A ALOHA SERIES
Darien Hsu Gee, Series Editor

Hali‘a Aloha ("cherished memories") by Legacy Isle Publishing is a guided memoir program developed in collaboration with series editor Darien Hsu Gee. The series celebrates moments big and small, harnessing the power of short forms to preserve the lived experiences of the storytellers. To become a Hali‘a Aloha author, please visit www.legacyislepublishing.net.

Legacy Isle Publishing is an imprint of Watermark Publishing, based in Honolulu, Hawai‘i, and dedicated to "Telling Hawai‘i's Stories" through memoirs, corporate biographies, family histories and other books.

© 2022 Adrienne Robillard

All rights reserved. No part of this book may be reproduced in any form or by any electronic or mechanical means, including information retrieval systems, without prior written permission from the publisher, except for brief passages quoted in reviews.

Tour diaries were previously published online in a different format at citizenshereandabroad.com.

All photos courtesy of the author.

ISBN 978-1-948011-78-5 (print)
ISBN 978-1-948011-79-2 (ebook)

Design and production
Dawn Sakamoto Paiva

Legacy Isle Publishing
1000 Bishop St., Ste. 806
Honolulu, HI 96813
Telephone 1-808-587-7766
Toll-free 1-866-900-BOOK
www.legacyislepublishing.net

Printed in the United States

CONTENTS

Intro: A Soundtrack	1
I. 1988–1991	
An Exception to the Rule	4
Heavy Metal Teacher	6
Aloha Tower	8
Highway 99	9
Mixtapes	12
Electric	14
Fresno Garage Band, 1991	16
Dream Job	19
Airfare	21
Transatlantic	22
Derbyshire	25
Senior Year	27
II. 1992-1996	
A Special New Band	30
Hull	33
Fever	37
One Night Band	40
Maps and Tapes	42
Rock 'n' Roll After Midnight	44
Ursula	45
Dough	47
III. 1996-2006	
Drummer Wanted	52
How to Play to an Empty Room	56

Rolling Tape	57
In the Same Space	59
Twelve Guys and One Woman in a Seedy Motel Off the 101	62
Debut	64
The Road to Texas	66
Tour Diary: SXSW, March 15, 2004	69
Tour Diary: Fresno, March 27, 2004	70
Accommodations	72
Brooklyn at 3:00 a.m.	75
Only the Clothes on Our Backs	78
Jobs Between Tours	80
White Transit Van	82
Saxmundham	84
Venue Architecture	86
Days Off	88
Overnight Ferry	89
Copenhagen	90
Hessle	92
Home	94
Signs of a Promising Show	96
The Great American	98
Brothers in Space	100
Last Leg	101
What I Wish I Knew Before Touring	104
Playlist	106
Coda	109
Acknowledgements	110

INTRO: A SOUNDTRACK

In the summer of 1986, my dad bought me a tape—the soundtrack to *Pretty in Pink*—at the Tower Records by Ala Moana Center. I'd recently watched *The Breakfast Club* at his house, mesmerized by the teenage world I saw on my own horizon. The ten songs on the soundtrack tape ushered me into seventh grade in a new school, in a new town, a new state, with new faces and new slang. My mother had moved us from Kailua, Hawai'i, to Fresno, California, and I went from having friends and blending in to being a loner who kept getting asked, "What are you?" because I was one of a few half-Asian students at Ahwahnee Middle School. With my headphones on, I could ignore uncomfortable questions.

Songs by the Smiths, New Order, Orchestral Manoeuvres in the Dark, the Psychedelic Furs, Suzanne Vega, and Echo and the Bunnymen provided refuge from a mainland world I felt I would never fit into. Each track opened a new door, leading me to more music. At Target in Fresno, the bright orange cover of the Smiths' *Louder Than Bombs* called to me, and its twenty-four songs played on auto-reverse until the batteries in my Walkman died. I found New Order's *Substance* at Sam Goody in Fashion Fair Mall and played it until the tape broke. In black pen I wrote band names and song lyrics on my blue school binder and along the soles of my Converse All-Stars, hoping these silent messages would pass through the fog of middle school to help me find anyone else who obsessively recorded *120 Minutes* on MTV at midnight on Sundays.

I.

1988–1991

AN EXCEPTION TO THE RULE

My mom signed me up for the youth group at University Presbyterian Church, where she had joined the Sunrise Singles group.

"I don't want to go," I said. One more place I wouldn't fit in.

"Just give it a try," my mom said.

My plan was to go once. But Craig and the other youth group leaders introduced me to bands like the Specials, the English Beat, and my favorite Fresno group, the Miss Alans. I went back. Craig sang in a band, the Town Criers, and he invited the youth group to his all-ages shows. Cindy, two years ahead of me in high school, had her driver's license, and she lived near me. We saw the Town Criers play with touring bands like the Mummies, going early for the sound check.

That year I was grounded for staying overnight at my friend Jenny's when her parents were out of town. The neighbors called the police because a bunch of kids came over and things got wild. But my mom let me go see the Replacements at Fresno State's Satellite College Union because Craig had already bought tickets for a few kids from youth group, including me. I got as close as I could to the stage, my heart beating quickly. The Replacements had a video on MTV's *120 Minutes* and I was seeing them live, in person, my one night of freedom before more weeks of being grounded.

The Replacements barely held it together. Any one of them could fall off the stage at any moment. I watched in awe as they just pulled through, finishing each song by a thread. It was exactly how my life felt.

I had to learn to play the guitar.

Student ID, freshman year; Fresno, California

HEAVY METAL TEACHER

My goal was to be in a touring band. But the furthest I went with the nylon-stringed guitar my mom bought me for Christmas was half a mile from my house to Patrick's Music on First and Barstow.

My guitar teacher wore very tight jeans, and I envied the way he got his hair to feather. I carried my guitar in a black cardboard case that I decorated with Smiths and New Order stickers purchased at Penny Candy, a store where an oversize cotton T-shirt bearing the son of God's face hung in view of shoppers with a bubble quote that read, "Don't shoplift. Jesus is watching you."

At thirteen I wanted to appear magically at movie theaters without anyone seeing my mom drop me off. In the same vein, I wanted to secretly learn to play guitar, without any witnesses, but one wall of the music lesson room was made of glass.

"Do you know 'Stairway to Heaven'?" my teacher asked.

I shook my head, hiding behind a veil of long, dark, permed hair.

"Led Zeppelin?" he said.

"Not really."

The teacher played the complicated song repeatedly while I admired his hair. But the last thing I wanted to do was play guitar in front of another human being, especially this man. In my bedroom I practiced the first position chord shapes I was assigned each week while listening to tapes on my dual cassette Sears stereo, forcing my fingers to press down the nylon strings. Eventually I moved from E major to C major to A minor. My teacher showed me how to tune my guitar. I broke a string, bought a new pack, and restrung it. After two months of guitar lessons, I could put three chords into a progression, the beginning of a song.

ALOHA TOWER

I took my guitar with me to Hawaiʻi for the summer when I stayed at my dad's, spending hours playing chords, going up and down the guitar neck, breaking strings.

The summer after my freshman year of high school I took the bus over the Pali to see the Red Hot Chili Peppers play at Aloha Tower. My friend Nicki and I intentionally arrived hours before the show. We stood outside with dozens of others who, like us, were broadcasting the bands they liked by wearing T-shirts featuring groups like New Order, Nine Inch Nails, and the Cult.

John Frusciante, the band's new guitarist, was a teenager like us. The Red Hot Chili Peppers danced on the edge of catastrophe like the Replacements, their show unpredictable, exciting, and loud.

The acoustic music I played sounded nothing like the controlled chaos of the Red Hot Chili Peppers or the other bands I was into, but I was getting better at guitar, maybe good enough to be in a band someday.

HIGHWAY 99

The 99 was an escape hatch from the grid of Fresno streets and the repeating storefronts: Vons, Save Mart, Carl's Jr., Fosters Freeze, Denny's, Taco Bell, Winchell's Donuts, Kentucky Fried Chicken, house after house after house, intersection after intersection. Cindy drove a Volkswagen Bug, the motor so loud we couldn't hear one another speak, our only option to gaze out the windows at an occasional freight train in the distance and the Oberti Olives sign over the San Joaquin River.

We listened to tapes and KFSR, broadcasting from Fresno State, until its signal wavered and we knew to turn around and go back. All the stuff flying through my head—how to quit obsessively playing my brother's Super Mario Brothers game when nobody else was home, how to get my mom to stop smoking, how to sew a giant bag that could hold all my tapes, how to write a really good song, how to avoid spending my whole summer on an island far away from the rest of my life because of a custody agreement—left me alone as long as there was music and space.

From the freeway, the San Joaquin River looked like a painting, cattails rising from where the water allowed them to grow. We passed the Mammoth Orange stand in Madera County, and the rows of crops in fertile fields and decaying old farmhouses created music videos for the songs blasting from the stereo—R.E.M., the Smiths, U2, and local bands like Let's Go Bowling. The music and motion were as reliable as the thick tule fog that turned the entire sky gray in winter and the heat mirages that wavered over the road in the distance in the summer.

The 99 was the way out of Fresno and the way back in. Years later I wrote song lyrics about it.

Out of the Valley

41 bleeds into 99, got enough gasoline and time.
Apostrophe. Is it yours or mine?
"Hey lady, can you spare a dime?"
Count the diesels, every one.
I will follow at twenty-one.
The strange quiet when the party ends.
The room empties. I begin again.
It's easy to be lazy in front of a computer screen.
Forty hours, five thousand calories.
Out of the valley the center of it all.

Secadora 7" record on Little Echoes, 2000

MIXTAPES

When we were back in Hawai'i for the summer stretch, my brother Terry and I paid a quarter each to ride TheBus into Honolulu from Kailua with a transfer to Waikīkī. At Tower Records and Jelly's Records & Tapes I discovered the British magazines *New Musical Express* and *Melody Maker* in the free bin because they were so outdated.

While my dad and stepmom were at work at the University of Hawai'i, Terry and I wandered the narrow pathways at the old International Marketplace in Waikīkī, abusing the free samples offered at the frozen yogurt stand until the people working there cut us off. I read every printed word in the music magazines, even the classified ads in the back, including a listing for a UK pen pal agency. Within a month, letters stamped with the queen's profile began to show up in my mailbox, along with ephemera sent by distant new friends: passport photos, tickets from shows like the Stone Roses on Spike Island. David mailed me mixtapes with new sounds: PJ Harvey, Galaxy 500, the Field Mice, Inspiral Carpets, Ned's Atomic Dustbin, Pulp, Suede, Blur, the Wedding Present, Ride, and Slowdive.

I called KFSR, the Fresno State University radio station, to request songs so I could record them. Just as David shared his soundtrack of England, I created a Fresno soundtrack, including songs from the bands I saw at all-ages shows like Melvins, Living Colour, Primus, lots of reggae and local bands like Let's Go Bowling, Reaction, and the Miss Alans. I stood in line at the post office with a completed green customs form to send tapes and letters to David in Wingerworth, Chesterfield, Derbyshire, his address much longer than mine.

Instead of holding everything in and pretending to be normal, like I did in my everyday life, I was honest with David. I told him I didn't want to go to Hawai'i for the entire summer. I told him how close I was with my younger brother, Terry, because we spent so much time traveling between Fresno and Hawai'i together. I often stopped my family story there because it was complicated, but I wrote about my two other brothers, one thirteen years older than me and one twelve years younger, from my parents' other marriages. I told him how my dad and stepmom were in the process of formally adopting my sister, Zandra, whom I had met in the Philippines when I was ten, before my stepmom's sister was no longer able to raise her.

David wrote that he and his younger brother were adopted and not biologically related to their parents or one another. With every letter it became clear that we were on opposite sides of the planet trying to figure out our lives in many of the same ways, playing guitar, writing letters, and writing music.

ELECTRIC

My grandparents drove to Fresno monthly, bringing Red Vines candy and Chinese treats like Khong Guan egg rolls in a metal tin, taking us to Fresno's different Chinese restaurants to find "the best one." Uncle Victor, Aunt Fran, and their kids drove through Fresno from Fremont in their RV, and we joined them on fishing trips. My cousin Jeff came to Fresno to visit his girlfriend, Adelina, who was a student at Fresno State. When I was fifteen, he carried an electric guitar and a Peavey practice amp from his truck into our living room.

"Your mom said you're learning to play," he said.

The guitar was a wood grain copy of a sort of 1970s style. The amp had a built-in fuzz feature that I loved. My new guitar teacher, Tom, taught me the blues and the pentatonic scales and introduced me to a shop that sold guitar effects pedals in Fresno's Tower District. I bought a Mosrite Fuzzrite and a digital delay pedal. With the fuzz pedal, even single notes became bulbous and round, covering up any errors with a shield of noise. The digital delay enabled me to make notes and chords echo and repeat, essentially turning me into two guitar players.

On weekday mornings my mom took my brother to school. With the house to myself, I turned my amp to volume ten and created different combinations of sound. I lost track of time and showed up at school after the late bell rang, but Mr. Volkmann, the school librarian, was in Sunrise Singles with my mom at church. He kindly wrote me a pass to avoid going to the office to be marked tardy.

"Why are you suddenly late all the time?" my friend Jon said. "You live closer to school than anyone I know."

When I told him he said, "I know a drummer named Arturo."

FRESNO GARAGE BAND, 1991

I knew who Arturo was. He sat next to me in geometry my freshman year and, like me, never said a word in class. One day when I glanced over at his desk, Arturo had created a mirror image likeness of himself with a No. 2 pencil on a sheet of white paper while the rest of us were barely awake plotting perpendicular lines.

Jon orchestrated an afternoon when he, Arturo, and Thomas, an exchange student from Norway, came over to my house after school, walking through the back field past the archery targets and the vernal pond that erupted with baby frogs each spring. I'd known Jon since middle school, but Arturo and Thomas were a grade ahead of us.

In Hawai'i we'd had an open carport, but in Fresno our garage was enclosed, like the houses on TV sitcoms. The drum kit my friend Jenny had let me borrow was set up against the back wall along with my guitar and amp. A collection of musical instruments recently retired from Fresno Unified School District, from finger castanets to an electric bass guitar that had an eagle carved into its body, was in the garage with a set of bongos and an autoharp, everything with

"FUSD" written or etched into it, things my mom had access to as a fourth grade public school teacher.

"Did you steal this stuff from the high school?" Thomas said.

"No." I stared at my feet.

Thomas studied the eagle bass. "Is there a strap?"

There wasn't, so he sat cross-legged on the concrete floor, plugged in, and started to play, as simple as chewing bubble gum. A lump formed in my throat. I was in over my head. Jon and Arturo were members of the Hoover High marching band. Thomas was in the orchestra elective, a multi-instrumentalist. I was taking art as my elective, making a starfish out of clay.

"I don't really know how to play the guitar," I said.

"Nonsense," Thomas said.

I turned my volume intentionally low. Arturo matched a beat to Thomas's bass line. Jon sat on the concrete floor leafing through one of my magazines. I tried not to look anyone in the eye as I tested out notes that might fit into the chord progression. But as anxious and unprepared as I felt playing guitar in front of other people, the current of energy that making music together created was addictive and worth all the risks I felt I was taking.

My mom popped her head into the garage. "We're going to have dinner in about a half hour." That meant Pizza Hut was on its way.

"See you at school," Jon said. They walked to his house a few blocks away.

Would they ever want to play music with me again? I was awkward and inexperienced. There were better guitar players at our high school and at every high school in Fresno.

But after a few weeks, we used the single mic on my boombox to record the songs we wrote. Thomas played keyboards and everything in the box of music instruments. Sometimes I filled in on bass guitar. After we captured a full song on tape, I drove us up and down Highway 41 in my mom's Nissan Sentra to listen to our stuff on the car stereo at full volume.

One day, Thomas and Arturo skipped school and left the valley, roaming San Francisco's Chinatown. That afternoon they came to my house still giddy from their adventure, eager to write a song about it. Jealous that they'd left Fresno without me, I wrote my own song about leaving.

Tambourine

I said that the city's not so far at all,
Not such a distance for you and me.
I can see the skyscraper lights more than they show me
    on TV.
You said you'd rather play the tambourine,
Sit on the back porch atmosphere of this place.
I'd agree on another day, but today I want some space.

Arturo Diaz, summer 1991; my mom's garage, Fresno, California

DREAM JOB

1. The clothes were provided. Even a hat.

2. My Taco Bell was in Clovis, beyond the orbit of my high school.

3. If I had a shift after my mom got home from work, I could drive there and listen to music.

4. The drive-thru headsets had a secret channel for employees to banter on to pass the time.

5. Taco Bell in the nineties opened at eight and closed by midnight.

6. There was a simple solution for everything: If we ran out of napkins, the manager sent me to Vons to buy some.

7. Free food at the end of every shift, including a Mexican pizza for my brother.

8. Music was piped in and on the playlist were bands like Blur.

9. I could give my friends free sodas anytime.

10. I saved up enough money to buy a roundtrip ticket to England.

AIRFARE

Home alone at sixteen, I called a travel agent listed in the yellow pages.

"Roundtrip from Fresno to Manchester, New Hampshire?" the travel agent said.

"Manchester, England," I said. I was often mistaken for my mom when I answered our home phone and hoped I sounded like an adult for this conversation.

There was clicking on the travel agent's keyboard. "I can sell you tickets on Virgin Atlantic. Or United. Either way you'll have to fly United out of Fresno."

Each time Terry and I shuttled back and forth from Fresno to Honolulu, we boarded United prop planes in the foggy Central Valley either on Christmas Eve or Christmas Day, depending on which parent had custody for the actual holiday. We arrived in Honolulu overdressed and sweaty, and wore slippers on the flight home only to have our toes freeze. Until I turned thirteen, old enough to commandeer us without an airline chaperone, Terry and I spent layovers at LAX and SFO in employee break rooms, sitting cross-legged on plastic chairs staring at a tiny TV watching *Cagney & Lacey* and *Mike Hammer* reruns.

There was more clicking. "The tickets will be ready for you to pick up and pay for on Thursday."

TRANSATLANTIC

I wrote my mom an essay making the case to go to England.

1. After five years of flying back and forth to Hawai'i, I was a seasoned traveler.

2. The custody agreement created when I was eleven no longer made sense at sixteen.

3. I would cover 100% of my travel expenses with the money I'd made.

4. I would be careful.

5. I would come back.

My mom sighed. "I don't want you to go. But I think you're going anyway."

As the plane began its descent through the clouds I saw neat rows of brick homes, architecture that matched what I'd seen on shows like *The Young Ones* and in films like *Life Is Sweet*. I'd read Frommer's and Let's Go travel books cover-to-cover, had memorized the populations of Manchester and Leeds and a brief history of the Edinburgh Castle.

The pins and needles in my legs disappeared as Heathrow swallowed me whole. Everywhere I stood someone seemed to ask, "Are you in the queue?" I didn't know the answer.

I wanted to call my mom from the many British Telecom pay phones, but I didn't have any coins, just stiff paper money and the American Express Travelers Cheques my mom had helped me buy. At the customs kiosk I faced a stoic agent in an official uniform.

"How long will you be in the UK?" he said.

"Ten days."

He stamped my passport. With sweaty palms, I waited for my luggage and looked at the single blurry photograph I had of David. He wore baggy jeans and a white and green T-shirt as he stood outside under light snowfall. I studied the photo, the traces of fingerprints showing in the light, unsure if I'd be able to identify him. My brother, Terry, had taken a clear photo of me at Sandy Beach a few months before my sixteenth birthday. I'd sent it to David.

I pushed my trolley into the arrivals area. A family gasped when the people they were looking for emerged, and I watched them laugh and hug one another. A tall young man stood alone holding a bouquet of flowers. Our eyes met. I pushed my trolley in his direction, ready to veer if he gave the bouquet to someone else.

"You're actually here," he said. I looked over my shoulder to confirm that he was talking to me. I accepted the flowers with shaking hands.

"I need to call my mom," I said. "Do you have any coins?"

David gave me all the pound coins he had in his pocket and showed me how to dial my phone number on the pay phone. He had memorized the country code from the handful of conversations we'd had.

"Adrienne," my mom said. "Be careful. Be smart."

DERBYSHIRE

The Harrisons' home was smaller than the 1960s ranch house I lived in with my mom and brother in Fresno. David's younger brother was out of town, and I was given the option of either sleeping on his twin bed in the room they shared or sleeping on "the settee in the lounge." Unsure what a "settee" or "lounge" was, and too shy to ask, I left my guitar and suitcase beside David's brother's bed. From his house we walked to the local pub to play pool and choose songs from the jukebox with his friends whose accents I could barely understand. I had stepped into a different life, a different world.

I wrote postcards to my mom, my brothers, my friends back in Fresno and Hawaiʻi, told them about how after Teenage Fanclub played at the Sheffield Leadmill a DJ took over and we danced for what felt like forever. After seeing Ride and Slowdive at the Slough Festival, we returned to David's relatives' locked house in London, the windows dark. We huddled together between their house and the neighbor's to try to stay warm for six hours until the sun came up, resting our heads on one another's shoulders, our fingers intertwined.

"Have you and your girlfriend been outside all night?" his great-aunt said when we finally rang the bell. "You should have woken me up."

We sat close to one another on the train ride back to Chesterfield, not mentioning my impending departure. During the layover in Los Angeles before my flight to Fresno I called my mom from a pay phone.

"Are you still a virgin?" she asked.

"Mom," I said.

"Well?"

"Yes."

SENIOR YEAR

Thomas had returned to Norway, but Arturo, who had graduated and now worked at one of the United Artists movie theaters, came over to write music for our new two-piece band. He played drums, I played guitar, and we alternated on vocals. We used my boombox to record tapes and drove around listening to our new songs: "Chapterhouse Rip-off," "Today (1)," "Today (2)," and the catchiest of all, "Hair." Sometimes our friend Kyle Oakes came over and played bass. Jon hung out.

David and I tried to sustain a long-distance relationship with letters and rare, expensive phone calls I paid for with Taco Bell dollars. He flew to California once and slept in the top bunk in my brother Terry's room but was stuck in Fresno without a driver's license and a bus system limited by car culture while I was at school.

I graduated from high school and no longer felt tethered to Fresno or Hawai'i. David bought tickets for us to go to the Reading Festival. I gave notice at Taco Bell and flew to England. For two weeks we existed in the same time zone, the same country, camping in Newquay and Reading, seeing Nirvana and dozens of other bands in the pouring rain.

II.

1992-1996

A SPECIAL NEW BAND

Making my own way to England had been a big deal but leaving home for college felt bigger. From my dorm room at UC Santa Barbara, I heard waves crash at night and in the morning I spotted seals on the sand soaking up the sun, but I was lonely. Other freshmen wandered in and out of the dorms introducing themselves, hanging out, meeting up in the dining halls and around campus. I felt like part of me was in England, part of me in Santa Barbara.

When my roommate was out, I listened to music alone on the dual cassette stereo my mom had given me as a graduation gift. A few weeks into the quarter, my friend Julie from high school offered a ride to Fresno, and I said yes, eager to return to someplace familiar, and she blasted Garth Brooks and Billy Ray Cyrus the whole way.

My mom filled the fridge with my favorite foods and brought home a flat of Costco muffins. But more than the food, I had missed my brother hovering in my doorway saying random things, my cat curling up on the edge of my bed, my mom knowing what mood I was in before I said a word.

"Have you looked into forming a band there?" she asked. "Maybe you can make a flyer this weekend. Post it around campus when you get back."

I spent the next two hours creating a flyer, not including any personal information about myself, listing only names of bands I liked: Jane's Addiction, Slowdive, Ride, the Stone Roses, the Smiths, and Poi Dog Pondering, just to see if anyone else knew who they were. I printed my dorm phone number on rip-off tags on the bottom. When I returned to UCSB I taped the flyer to poles and bulletin boards on and off campus.

A day later I came back from class and my roommate said, "You have five messages."

One guy played the bass to every song from Jane's Addiction's *Nothing's Shocking* while I stood in his living room, my guitar slung over my shoulder, hoping he would stop.

Two guys named Dan called and I went to their apartment. Blond Dan L. used guitar pedal effects to make motorcycle sounds while Dan K., who was hapa like me, sat on a motorbike cushion pretending to ride a chopper. They were weird in the best ways.

"What bands on the flyer do you like?" I asked.

"Poi Dog Pondering," Dan K. said.

"I didn't see the flyer," Dan L. said.

The Dans' friend Jordan set up his drum kit in their living room. I plugged in my guitar and amp and played "Tambourine" for them. The guys played along. It was our first song.

I signed us up for an open mic night on campus by the dorms. After a series of Indigo Girls cover duos, we took the stage. Our guitars were not acoustic. We had amps and drums. Were we too loud? Would the sound guy turn us off? We did not fit in. But we were oddballs together. Whatever happened would happen to all of us.

A few friends I'd made in the dorms moved toward the stage. Friends of the guys in the band hollered our name: "Boot Cookies!"

For two years, we played every show we were offered in the daylight and in the dark. The only time I missed band practice was when I got the chicken pox. David and I broke up, ending our expensive and agonizing late night and early morning phone calls. Instead of writing letters, I wrote songs with the Boot Cookies, stopping only when I left the country to study in the UK.

HULL

In September 1994, I flew from Fresno to LAX to join two dozen other students from University of California campuses. We boarded a Virgin Atlantic flight to London, underage Americans suddenly of legal drinking age on the plane and on the ground.

My friend DH and I saw Ride at the Royal Albert Hall before he headed for the University of Birmingham. I took the train north from King's Cross Station, lugging my suitcase, backpack, and the electric guitar I'd bought in Santa Barbara after the one my cousins loaned me caught fire at the Dans' apartment.

Student ID, 1994-1995; Hull, England

Rob, an American from North Carolina, was sitting in the living room of my temporary student orientation flat. After I got settled, we walked to the student union pub on campus. Everyone seemed to wear black or dark clothing, jeans, and scarves, a stark contrast from the colorful surfwear and T-shirts students wore at UCSB.

"It feels like we've traveled back in time here," Rob said. "Milk is delivered in bottles by the milkman."

"I was told that it's socially unacceptable for women to buy a full pint of beer here," I said.

"Watch out for the Americans breaking weird beverage rules," Rob said.

We walked up the many stairs to the student pub and stepped inside. David, his girlfriend, and his friends were sitting at a booth near the door. I knew that he was a student there but didn't expect to run into him on the first day. Like a moth to flame, I went over to say hello, hoping to not seem crazy for suddenly reappearing in his world. I could have avoided the situation completely if I had just chosen to study in Glasgow, Essex, Norwich, Birmingham, or Edinburgh, anywhere but Hull.

After an awkward conversation I rushed over to the bar to order a full pint of beer. "How do you know people here already?" asked a mystified Rob.

"Two years ago, he was my boyfriend."

Rob nodded. "Did you come here hoping you'd get back together?"

"Maybe. Is that sad?"

He shook his head. I appreciated his understanding my predicament and not asking any questions when I suggested we ditch the student union after downing our drinks.

I was there. For a whole year. I couldn't go home. I had to make the most of it. One day, David's girlfriend, Bronwen, approached me on campus and said, "I grew up moving a lot and know how it is to be in a new place and not know anyone. Well, you know David," she laughed. She and I are still friends today, almost thirty years later, though David moved to Japan sometime in the late nineties and we lost touch.

Letters from home buoyed me when I was at risk of drowning in homesickness, wondering why I had ever left the warm Santa Barbara sunshine for the everlasting cold of Northern England, why I had put so much distance between myself and the Boot Cookies, why I had ever thought that I could live in another country for a whole year. My friends Jamie, Laurel, Kerri, Rob O., Chrissy, Jeff, Steve, and Brad wrote, as did my brothers, Terry and Tom. My mom wrote me the most, keeping me afloat through the year, through the ups and downs and self-doubt. My dad sent me emails that I read and responded to at the computer center on campus. My grandmother wrote as well. She always signed her letters "Love, Grandpa and Grandma," but I could hear her voicing every word.

Nov. 15-1994

Dear Adrienne,

How are you? Is it getting pretty cold now in England? You've been gone over 2 months. Are you getting use to things yet? Next week will be Thanksgiving. We all will be at Victor's. Shirley & Tuatan will stay home. We will miss you for Thanksgiving. One year is not that long. You will be home before you get too home sick. If you could use your time to learn as much as you can about their life style. That's part of the main reason for you to go abroad. Right?

It's so good to talk to you when we visit Lily & Terry. I am not a very good in writing letter. If you have time drop us a line. We are all doing well. Hope you are too.

Love
Grandpa + Grandma

Letter from Grandma Gin, November 1994

FEVER

"Blink your eyes so we know you're not dead." An American woman was speaking to me, but I knew I was in a youth hostel near St. Paul's Cathedral in London.

I blinked. I wasn't wearing contact lenses and I hoped my glasses were still in my backpack. My mouth was dry. I felt horrible.

"Are you okay?" the woman said.

"I got the flu."

The woman said, "I'm going to give you some Advil to break the fever." She gave me two tablets. "How long have you been in England?"

"Since September. I'm studying here." I swallowed the candy-coated pills.

She turned to speak to one of her friends, all of them blurry.

"Have you heard Dave Matthews? He's huge back in the States."

I nodded off. When I woke up again, they were gone, but she'd left a Dave Matthews tape on the edge of my bed. I slid the tape into my Walkman, replacing

Mudhoney, but nothing happened. The batteries had died.

After my fever broke, I showered, dug around in my backpack, found two more AA batteries, and made my way outside. At a Burger King I ate my first meal in days: a milkshake, fries, and a Whopper with cheese. I listened to Dave Matthews as I dipped my fries in ketchup, thinking, "This is what's happening in the US." That night, I returned the tape to the young woman. Feeling like a brand-new person, I bought the latest issue of *TimeOut* and took the Tube to meet Jamie, my college roommate from UCSB, at Heathrow.

We went to see Daisy Chainsaw play at the Water Rats in King's Cross. Their original female singer wasn't there and one of the guys stepped up to do vocals. I wanted to ask them if I could audition to be their singer, but I didn't, because the guy was really good. Jamie and I took in the show like we did at clubs like the Anaconda back in Isla Vista and then talked about it afterward in depth. I wished she was staying longer than a week.

"I see the Dans sometimes," Jamie said. "Jordan too."

"I sent Dan L. an aerogram. But he didn't write back."

"I'm sure he liked receiving it."

Two nights later we saw Stereolab play at the Irish Centre with Cornershop and a few other bands. The venue was cozy, and warmth returned to my fingers and toes. As everything started to close for Christmas, Jamie and I took a train to Surrey to our friend Andy's house. The previous year, Andy had studied at UCSB on exchange from the University of Essex. He was a regular at Boot Cookies shows and a fellow musician.

On Christmas, Andy's dad generously offered, "Ring your family. Tell them Happy Christmas!"

My grandma came on the line. "Adrienne, are you wearing the sweaters I gave you?"

"Every day."

My grandma was at least four sizes smaller than me, but to help me stay warm in the UK, she'd given me wool sweaters she'd knitted for herself in the 1960s. Cut off from burritos and bagels and having taken up dancing until past midnight in indie nightclubs, I actually fit into the sweaters—mostly. The sleeves were a bit short and the collars were oversized, but I was grateful for the layer of wool.

"Are you eating Chinese food?" she said.

"Sometimes."

"Try to eat Chinese food, with vegetables. It's very healthy," my grandma said.

ONE NIGHT BAND

At the University of Hull, I joined the Musician's Exchange, a club for aspiring musicians, and at the first meeting, I met Matt. We were both nineteen, our birthdays the same month of the same year, and both new to Hull. He came from Wales. I borrowed a drum kit from the Musician's Exchange and carted it to my house on Cottingham Road. Matt played my sunburst Gibson Les Paul. On afternoons when we should have been studying, we figured out song parts and strung them together.

At the Adelphi Club on De Grey Street, less than a mile from the university, Monday was open mic night. There was no cover at the door—leaving pound coins in student pockets for pints of cider, beer, and crisps. But it wasn't a student venue, per se. Anyone could perform, so going there was unpredictable and fun. You never knew who would walk onto the stage or what they might do.

Matt and I signed up with a plan to play one song, maybe two if we could bleed them together, if we could even last that long. I had one pint of beer and then two. Paul, owner of the Adelphi, set up a mic for me by the floor tom. It was all chaos. It was fun. Loud. And it only happened once. But it wasn't the same as being in a regular band like the Boot Cookies. Nobody else was like Dan L., and they'd all graduate before I returned to Santa Barbara.

MAPS AND TAPES

After taking my exams with fingers crossed, I shipped everything I couldn't fit into my travel backpack to the US and said goodbye to my friends and the student flat where the lack of regular hot shower water had led me to cut my hair Pat Benatar short. With a copy of the European youth hostel guide, my Walkman and tapes, and the 1995 summer train timetable, thick as a Bible, I met Kerri in Amsterdam. We spent the next month traveling by train from Oslo to Corfu, cherishing rare, iced beverages and learning why Canadians don their national flag to avoid being mistaken as Americans.

Friends since we were six, Kerri and I indulged in long conversations that international phone calls didn't allow. We sampled and evaluated each country's version of Marie biscuits and hot dogs. In Malmö a group of nine young Swedish men tried to convince us to go home with them from the train station until the station manager locked them out and locked us in. When invited to party on the top level of a ferry bound for Corfu we turned to one another, confessing that we both preferred the calm below, away from the crowds of other twenty-somethings, relieved that we weren't disappointing one another.

In my overstuffed backpack, I had everything I needed for thirty days of travel, but I soon wished I'd brought more tapes. I didn't have the money to buy new ones or the space to carry them. Kerri's cassettes added variety to the songs imprinted on my brain. I studied the maps in the youth hostel book and the train guide. Our goal was to see as many places as possible.

The brown rolling hills and heat in southern Europe made me look forward to going home to California, being reunited with my entire music collection, the highways, places, and people I knew. As we boarded trains bound for Prague, Lyon, and Barcelona, I realized that no matter how much I loved to travel, going home was going to be sweet.

One night in Spain, Kerri said, "You talk about Dan L. a lot. Will he be in Santa Barbara when you get back?"

"I doubt it," I said.

"I hope he's there," Kerri said. "I can tell how much he means to you."

I didn't realize I was talking about him so much.

ROCK 'N' ROLL AFTER MIDNIGHT

Amaya and I met in trigonometry my junior year at Hoover High when she was an exchange student from Madrid. Because I hung out with her and played music with Thomas from Norway, the year they left some kids at school asked me, "Why are you still here?"

I often wondered the same question.

Before returning to the US at the end of that summer in 1995 I drove with Amaya and her boyfriend from Madrid to Avila where their band, Venus Pluton, performed. Watching them come together in that town on the hill in the middle of the night to play their music, I knew that as soon as I got back to UCSB, I had to be part of a band. I wasn't sure how or with whom, but I needed it more than burritos, bagels, and peanut butter.

URSULA

While I was in England, Dan K. moved back to Orange County, and Jordan, the Boot Cookies' drummer, graduated with a marine biology degree and returned to San Diego where he'd grown up. I resumed my old job at the student post office before the fall quarter began. A few days later, standing in the customer service window, Dan L. said, "Hey. Wanna play music?"

"I thought you graduated," I said.

He shook his head. "Not yet."

I'd sold my electric guitar in England to help pay for my train pass, so I bought a cheap bass guitar in Ventura. Dan and I met in a tiny rehearsal space in Isla Vista to figure out song parts, piecing them together. Somebody stored a drum kit there, which we took turns playing. Dan played guitar and I played bass and wrote lyrics. We recorded songs onto a four-track. Writing songs together felt electric.

Staying up late in the windowless rehearsal space, we caught up on the last year of our lives, including people we'd dated and bands we'd seen. When Sonic Youth and the Foo Fighters had shows in LA, we went together. Driving the 101 to LA and back, listening to music, I realized why I'd missed Dan so much. He just got me. We'd both moved to similar parts of California in the seventh grade, him to Upland, in San Bernardino County, from Pennsylvania, and me to Fresno from Hawai'i. We could talk a lot or not at all. We could write songs. We went out on a date.

Jamie introduced us to a solid drummer, CT. With him we played shows in downtown Santa Barbara and Storke Plaza on campus. We named our group Ursula after one of the characters in *Women in Love* by D. H. Lawrence. The week of graduation we played parties before I flew to Hawai'i for the summer. Dan went home to Upland, uncertain of what the future might bring. He bought a plane ticket to meet me in Hawai'i in July.

DOUGH

I was twenty-one years old with a degree in literature and I was sharing a bedroom with my youngest brother, Tom, who was eight. He talked about basketball as he nodded off to sleep on the top bunk and I lay awake on the bottom, wondering what to do with my life.

At Kailua Beach I read Douglas Coupland's *Generation X: Tales for an Accelerated Culture*, a graduation gift, and in the shade of the dogwood trees I dozed off. Kerri was back in Hawai'i for a pharmacy internship, and she picked me up after work in her dad's truck. Few music groups I was into played Hawai'i, but that summer we saw Love and Rockets perform at a warehouse in Iwilei. They blew me away, the band so tight and exact. The Jesus and Mary Chain played a small club in Waikīkī, and we stood near the front, getting blasted by sound.

My dad suggested that I sign up with a temp agency in Honolulu. I took TheBus to town and answered telephones at a foster care placement agency for one day. I counted the number of cars that took the University exit off the H-1. In the shade of a monkey pod tree, I avoided the clusters of ants whose territory I'd invaded, my headphones on at full volume as I marked tallies on a sheet.

Living at my dad's house had its ups and downs, so for more personal space I moved in with Kerri and her dad, the one major rule being that when *Masterpiece Theater* was on, there was no changing the channel.

I worked the Sbarro pizza counter at the Royal Hawaiian shopping center to save up money for a rental car when Dan came out. Bubba and his cousin twirled pizza dough in the stand-alone hut on the ground floor while their young wives from Japan organized the plastic forks, knives, and napkins.

The national car rental agencies required a hefty fee from drivers under the age of twenty-five, but a place off Nimitz rented to me for less. I picked Dan up at the airport, parking the Chevrolet Beretta in the short-term lot and running barefoot to meet him at the gate. Mosquitos devoured us at a youth hostel in Waimea as we ate a Pizza Hut pie out of a box in our room. In the Beretta we moved between campsites at Kahana Bay and Waimānalo Beach, eating hot dogs we grilled and sleeping like sardines in the tiny, child-size tent Cindy had given me as a graduation gift. At Hanauma Bay we snorkeled beyond the reef to where the water is deep, we swam in the pool below Sacred Falls, watched movies at Kam Drive-In, and ate cheap plate lunches. We splurged on a meal at the Hard Rock Cafe and a sunset cruise I booked from a pay phone on a kamaʻāina discount. We had enough money to stay in a Waikīkī hotel for one night.

Dan flew back to California, and I left the Islands for Fresno. A few weeks later we met up in San Francisco, signed up with temp agencies, and started looking for a drummer.

III.

1996-2006

DRUMMER WANTED

I drove from Fresno over the Bay Bridge in my mom's Volvo and circled the blocks around Jackson and Leavenworth to park outside the apartment I'd be sharing with my cousin, Tristan. Dan often stayed at my place because he worked in the financial district, a few minutes away on the 1 California bus or a fifteen-minute walk downhill through Chinatown.

We placed ads for a drummer in the *Guardian* and the *SF Weekly*. A guy in his thirties who lived with his mom stated, "I love T. Rex!" like a confession between songs. We played with a college friend's friend in a Potrero Hill rehearsal space soundproofed with defective plush animals stapled to the walls and ceilings.

At night Dan and I went to see bands play at the Paradise Lounge, the Cocodrie, the Bottom of the Hill, the Purple Onion, and the Tip Top Inn, drinking pints of beer while we absorbed the sounds of the city. Muni's unreliability and our lack of a car or taxi money meant that we walked to many shows, following the bus routes. We used temp job paychecks to buy tickets to see Blur, Supergrass, Pavement, Weezer, and Lush at the Warfield and Fillmore.

Charles was at the Guitar Center when we posted a flyer there. He had also just graduated from college and lived in a studio in the Tenderloin. After playing with us for a month he decided to relocate to a shared flat in the same building I had moved to in the Haight, around the corner from Dan's new place.

With Charles on drums, we rented an eight-by-eight-foot room at a place called Rockers on Grace Avenue in SOMA run by a guy named John Rocker who also owned and operated a music shop around the corner. In that part of the city, we witnessed drug deals and homelessness while the city boomed with jobs and tech money. We named our group Secadora and recorded demos on my four-track. Dan called bookers on his lunch break. When we got a chance to open for other bands, we made show flyers and stapled them to telephone poles, invited our friends and everyone we knew at work. Charles helped get Secadora off the ground, but Dan and I were looking for harder hits on the snare, something steadily menacing.

We ran new ads in the weeklies. When I came home from work and the light on the answering machine was blinking, I wondered if the person we were looking for even existed. We were looking for someone who:

1. Had their own taste in music but liked some of the same bands we did.

2. Wouldn't flake on band practice, always helped with load-in or load-out for shows, and never borrowed money. At least not too often.

3. We could hang out without becoming super annoyed.

4. We'd feel OK sharing a hotel room with. And a bathroom, specifically, a toilet.

5. Had similar goals. Becoming the Tuesday night band at the Irish pub wasn't our wish.

Christian showed up with his boyfriend, who sat cross-legged on the floor for the entire audition. Tall, with dark hair, Christian came across as serious, sat down behind the drum kit, and we started playing part of a song. He was on time, with precision, using the ride cymbal, one of our unspoken requirements. He took a bus across the Golden Gate Bridge to practices, eventually moving to San Francisco with his cat. Encouraged by finding an awesome drummer, we placed an ad for a bass player. After several awkward auditions, Chris S. showed up. He instantly felt familiar, and he'd been to many of the same shows as us. We practiced on weeknights after work, went to shows, and recorded a new demo on a four-track at Chris S.'s house in the Sunset. Dan booked us a show at the Bottom of the Hill, the best indie club in San Francisco. But having a show didn't mean there would be an audience.

Dan Lowrie, Adrienne Robillard, Chris Scholz, Christian Serra, Secadora promo picture, 1998

HOW TO PLAY TO AN EMPTY ROOM

1. Close your eyes.

2. Turn your back to the empty space and face your band. Even with nobody there, you're getting better at playing out.

3. Enjoy some beverages before you take the stage, but not too many.

4. If there's a mirror behind the bar and you like the way you look, watch yourself.

5. Practice new songs you've never played out before because being in a different space will help to fine tune the parts and prepare you for the next show.

ROLLING TAPE

John Vanderslice of the band MK Ultra ran Tiny Telephone Studios in San Francisco. For two days and nights over a Fourth of July weekend we recorded five songs on two-inch tape with engineer Rick Stone, staying into the small hours, after everyone's deodorant had stopped working. Fireworks exploded on the Fourth and made it onto the recording, buried in the background. We stopped only to eat lunch across the street at Papa Potrero's Pizza where a taxidermy dog watched us with glass eyes. Rick made rough cassette mixes that we listened to in my Honda, fine tuning the dramatic layers of each song. My head was spinning at the end of the two days, and I was both exhausted and thrilled.

Dan's brother, Matt, designed the cover artwork. Mr. Toad's Recording duplicated the CDs that Dan and I mailed to every club on the West Coast and dozens of indie record labels, looking for a home. We played shows in LA at Al's Bar, the Martini Lounge, and the Garage, where my underage brother, Terry, and his friends snuck in during the soundcheck. We hooked a U-Haul trailer to Chris's Ford Explorer and toured the Pacific Northwest supporting the Lo-Fi Neisans, from Japan, and the Get Go, friends of ours from San Francisco. At Portland's Satyricon we played with Arturo's band, Tennis, and slept in Kerri's living room beside her pet chinchilla. In a Seattle dive bar on Second Street some drunk old guys alternated between yelling at us to quit and never stop.

But bands, like all relationships, change over time. Chris left to focus on his video game company. We continued as a three-piece with Christian and recorded the LP *Little Pieces of Paper* in 2001 at Tiny Telephone, playing shows at the Silverlake Lounge in LA and at our favorite venues in San Francisco, including the Make Out Room. I bought a Danelectro guitar to cover the lower notes for bass.

IN THE SAME SPACE

Secadora shared a few different rehearsal studios with friends of ours—CW, Chris G., and Jane—who were in a band called Dealership. But practice spaces in San Francisco were disappearing as loft housing was built, so both bands moved to Soundwave in West Oakland. Dan and I lined the walls with acoustic foam. I hung up an oversize *The Queen Is Dead* poster from my high school bedroom. Christian left and we played shows with Kjrsten on drums, but Secadora fizzled.

In 2001 Dan and I moved out of the city to an apartment in the Temescal area of Oakland, across the street from CW. After our friends' bands played shows, at least two or three nights a week, we'd go to the 7-Eleven on Fortieth Street and buy terrible junk food.

"Meat shouldn't come out of a pump," said CW.

"Sure is tasty though," Dan said.

"Are you guys going to start a new band?" CW asked.

I nodded. "After the wedding."

On a flight from Honolulu to San Francisco in 2001, our backpacks filled our carry-on bag space below the seats in front of us and there was no room to kneel. Dan reclined his chair, brought out a ring, proposed, and without reservation I said, "Yes." My mom and brother sat behind us, clapping.

We got married twice in the summer of 2002. The first ceremony was traditional—wedding dress, tuxedo, bouquets, and cake. It was officiated by CW in Oakland with Dan's family, my mom's side of my family, and many friends there. The song for our first dance was the Smiths' "There Is a Light that Never Goes Out." A week later we traveled to Hawai'i with five friends and my brother Terry, and were married at Kalama Beach Club in Kailua with my dad's side of the family and friends. Father Champion officiated, my brother Tom did a reading, and we all feasted on Filipino food prepared by my stepmom's family.

After our honeymoon, CW met us at the studio. I'd worked out the skeleton of a new song and I wanted to hear drums over the two chords I was plucking back and forth. Dan layered on guitar. We'd played the song with other drummers after Christian, but nobody had clicked with it like this.

With CW on drums, "You Drive" came together quickly. Chris G. joined us on bass and vocals. Citizens Here and Abroad began, the band's name inspired by Chapter 20 of my Aunt Shirley's 1950s Girl Scout handbook, which detailed how to be a good citizen. When I wasn't teaching GED test prep, ESL, or community college English, I was sending demos to clubs to book shows. This band was different from before. We'd been friends with CW and Chris G.

for over five years. Writing songs felt natural and the songs came quickly.

We practiced twice a week, three times if we had a show, but we knew the best way to really polish songs was to tour.

You Drive

You drive and we'll listen to music and the engine.

—Citizens Here and Abroad, *Ghosts of Tables and Chairs*

TWELVE GUYS AND ONE WOMAN IN A SEEDY MOTEL OFF THE 101

For the "Birds of a Feather Tour" in 2003, we headed south on the 101 in a caravan with our friends' bands Thee More Shallows and Film School. Citizens traveled in CW's late-1990s white Dodge Caravan where if one person ate a banana, everyone was smelling banana, and then banana peel, for miles as it turned from yellow to brown to mush.

The first venue: a savory pie shop in San Luis Obispo. The show was lightly attended, but there were thirteen musicians to fill in space and eat the free pies we received as payment. After the show we navigated to a motel off the 101. One of the three bands didn't pay for a room and crashed with the two other bands. I'm not going to say who. I woke early to be the first in the shower.

The next show was at Spaceland in Silverlake. With friends in LA, the audience was more robust than at the pie shop. It was like playing a show in San Francisco except the weather was warmer and there were more options for breakfast burritos the next morning.

How far could we go with this? Out of the state? Out of the country? We wanted to find out. But we needed to record and release a CD, we needed a label and a booking agent.

Dan taught himself Pro Tools and Logic and we recorded ten songs in our practice space early in the mornings before the classic rock cover and grindcore bands were there. The vocals were recorded in closets in our apartment on 40th Street in Oakland. It was less pressure and cheaper than booking time in a studio but just as fun to listen to each playback. Recording the vocals was especially fun with Chris G. Our voices bled together and then became distinct again.

With a full album of songs, we made CD duplicates and mailed them out to labels, fingers crossed.

Adrienne Robillard, Soundwave Studios, 2003

DEBUT

At an internet café in Waikīkī, Dan and I received an email from Mark Kaiser. His label, Omnibus Records, was interested in releasing Citizens Here and Abroad's debut CD, *Ghosts of Tables and Chairs*. This was big. Everything we'd recorded in previous bands, other than the 7-inch Secadora single with Little Echoes, had been self-released. Someone else saw the potential in our music to invest in album art, to print and distribute the CD, mail it to music publications, advertise. Omnibus was a cool label with the Shins, the Intelligence, Track Star, Mates of State, Electro Group—bands that were setting the tone of the early 2000s. And we found out later that Mark had been a student of my Aunt Shirley's in Ventura.

The album release date was February 3, 2004. Our friend Jason Koxvold filmed a video for the third track, "Appearances." The video shoot night was cold, and I felt awkward about taking over Jason's friends' space to lip synch through their yard, but the video opened doors for us.

The second video Jason shot was for "You Drive," the final track on *Ghosts of Tables and Chairs*. Jason hired a stuntman to drive and crash a classic Cadillac.

In the video it looks like the band is in the car when it flips, but I was behind the wheel of a different Cadillac, with Chris G. in the passenger seat and Dan and CW in the backseat. The stuntman had one chance to flip the car and he nailed it. A make-up professional, Dianna, coated my face with products I mostly wiped off, and a costume designer, Corey, chose clothing for us. The video was shot in Mission Bay in San Francisco when it still looked spooky and industrial, the ghost of the Esprit Outlet store lingering in the fog. Later, some kids at our shows in Newcastle, England, said they came to see us because they'd seen the "You Drive" video on MTV Europe.

Promo photo for *Ghosts of Tables and Chairs*, Omnibus Records, 2004. Left to right: Chris Groves, Dan Lowrie, Adrienne Robillard, Chris Wetherell

THE ROAD TO TEXAS

We just had to make it from California to the Lone Star State and back. The video for "Appearances" was being screened at the 2004 South by Southwest (SXSW) film festival, and we were booked to play.

The tour began at Spaceland in LA, small enough to fill up with friends. My college roommate Jamie and her friend Leslie joined us for a Thai dinner before the show. Other college friends showed up: Laurel, Jenny, Christine, Dan K., and Dianna. The next morning my left eye was itchy. We played a show at Sea Level Records that afternoon. Any non-club, non-nighttime show was awkward without the shadows to hide behind. But Eric's sister, Sylvia, stood right in front and got into the music so I did too. She's very tall and blocked just enough light to give the record store a mystique.

The day after the show, I drove myself to an urgent care facility in San Bernardino. A guy named Jim who was playing golf in the lobby was called in for an appointment before me. I was given a tiny tube of medicine for pink eye to put on the inside of my eyelids, but I touched the tip of the tube to my eye and contaminated the whole thing the second day. I called my Uncle Victor and Aunt Fran, the family optometrists.

They said, "The infection will resolve within a week. But don't wear contact lenses. Hopefully you can keep the infection to one eye."

In Tucson, Jonathan, a graduate student, and his girlfriend, Nicolette, interviewed us at the University of Arizona radio station studio before our show at Plush. I wore glasses, my eye weeping, and I was anxious about giving pink eye to everyone. We stayed with Jonathan in his studio apartment attached to his grandmother's home. She had at least eight tiny white dogs that barked whenever we were in the driveway. The next morning, I woke with both of my eyes glued shut. In the shower I unsealed my eyelids and tried to clean the shower stall as best as I could, rinsing every surface.

"I have pink eye," I told Jonathan.

"I know," he said with a shrug. "It's no big deal."

"Maybe bleach the shower or something," I said, envious of his low level of worry.

"I'm sure I won't get it." And he didn't. But back in California, Eric, Chris G.'s partner, did. (Sorry, Eric!)

With me as our booking agent, our itinerary was often random. In Phoenix we played the Emerald Lounge, next door to a place selling "wings and things." The headliner was a ska band named Spaz Kitty who sang "Happy Birthday" to Chris G. with enthusiasm. The next night we debated driving to the Grand

Canyon but decided to relax in Flagstaff at a motel listed in the AAA book. I hoped with some chill time my pink eye would resolve on its own, ideally within the next twenty-four hours, before we opened for the Decemberists in Albuquerque at the Launchpad. *Her Majesty the Decemberists* was on regular rotation in our tour van stereo.

While my eyes were clearer the next day, they were still too bloodshot for me to wear contacts. As opener Tom Heinl sang "Ingrown Nail (on the Oregon Trail)," I felt lucky to only have pink eye and be traveling in an automobile. The Decemberists' merch manager, Bernadette, and Chris, the guitarist, invited us to see them play SXSW.

The next night we played with our friends, Film School, at the Gypsy Tea Room in Dallas. After the soundcheck, we waited to see who would come. The bass player for Low Flying Owls explained how he'd burnt his eyebrows off on his stove by accident. The venue was mostly empty that night, but each band was paid a $200 guarantee, enough to cover a room at a Best Western and gas to get to Austin.

TOUR DIARY
SXSW, March 15, 2004

A young lady named Diedre asked me to get on the mic and ask her boyfriend, Shane, who was in the bar, to move to Austin, so I did, and we were invited to smoke and shoot guns after the show with them.

Left to right: Dan Lowrie, Adrienne Robillard, Chris Wetherell, Chris Groves

TOUR DIARY
Fresno, March 27, 2004

While I left the Central Valley at seventeen to go to college, there's something about that flat, quiet city of truck drivers and Costcos and mini malls, with all its parking and convenience, big blue sky and calm, that I dream about sometimes. My mom had a buffet set up for us when we arrived: veggies and dip, chips, a party platter from Bobby Salazar's, soda, beer, juice, water, cookies, and brownies. Then she decided to get a pizza too, so I went with her to Round Table, where during high school I often spent my lunch break for their $1.99 slice-and-soda special. The inside of RT had been remodeled, but it looked worse somehow, too bright, not dark like I remembered, a cave to retreat into between fourth and fifth periods.

Unlike Round Table, Tokyo Gardens was the same, four years after Dan and I played there with Secadora. Before the set, my friend Valerie's cousin, Bobby Lee, shared that "Fresno is *Esquire Magazine*'s number six city in the USA for live music." My mom had a front row seat and there was a good crowd.

After the show, I hoarded AAA maps, making the most of my membership for the rest of the *Ghosts of Tables and Chairs* tour. The first show was in Reno, with I Can Lick Any Son of a Bitch in the House. Their singer helped Chris G. file his taxes online. We continued onto Salt Lake City; Denver; Lawrence, Kansas; Norman, Oklahoma—the shows I booked making more sense on paper than on the map, the band getting tighter the further we drifted from home.

The four of us turned heads in West Virginia, our clothes unlike those of the other diners at a roadside stop. My and CW's vague ethnicities felt more pronounced when we were outside urban areas. We were often unshowered and carried overstuffed backpacks when we emerged from the 1990s white Dodge Caravan, keeping our valuables within reach, appearing strange. We looked sleepy and sloppy, but we always paid the bill.

Almost thirty years old, I still called my mom from pay phones when I could find them.

ACCOMMODATIONS

Dayton, Ohio, was where my grandpa first lived after arriving by ship from China in the 1930s, around age twelve, to join his father in America. Citizens Here and Abroad arrived in Dayton from Chicago on day seven of our US tour.

At the venue, Elbows and Chins, a bartender of ambiguous ethnicity poured us complimentary drinks. I felt like I could blend in. The neon lighting was straight out of Tech Noir, the club Sarah Connor goes to in *The Terminator*. Everything was cool. For a minute.

Via email, Dave, who was in one of the other bands and booked the show, had offered us a place to stay after the gig. I had accepted. But when we met, I realized he was a teenager. A feeling of dread came over me. What were the accommodations he had offered?

After the show we loaded our gear into the van.

"You guys up for going to Denny's?" Dave and his girlfriend, Amanda, asked.

It was the perfect opportunity to say there had been a miscommunication, we had booked a hotel.

An exit was within reach. A copy of the AAA Kentucky, Ohio and West Virginia TourBook was in the van.

But we said, "Sure." Dave and Amanda were so nice, we didn't want to be rude.

In the Dodge minivan, we followed Amanda's VW Bug to the twenty-four-hour diner.

"How long do you think we'll be here?" I asked.

"Too long," CW said.

The Denny's had the same floorplan as the one my grandpa owned in Fresno, but in Dayton there were ashtrays in the bathroom stalls.

"Why is everyone staring at us?" Dan said.

"We're in our thirties hanging out with teenagers after midnight," Chris G said.

"We're creepy," CW said. "And sweaty."

Dave and Amanda waved us over to their booth while strangers stared. We ordered food and lots of water.

Two hardcore goths entered the restaurant, taking a booth near ours, and thankfully the eyeballs shifted to them. Amanda played the toy grabbing game in the lobby until our limp sandwiches arrived. Around 2:30 a.m., we trailed the teens to Dave's parents' house, a sizable McMansion embedded in a cul-de-sac.

Dave pointed to a flat of muffins in the giant, unlit kitchen. "My parents got those for you guys from Costco."

Amanda and Dave went upstairs, and we took turns brushing our teeth in a nautical themed bathroom off the kitchen. Numerous framed family photos were arranged on shelves.

"Dave's parents are probably the same age as us," CW said, pointing at the pictures.

"Maybe even younger," Chris G. said.

"We could have a house like this," I said. "In Ohio."

"We could have a son who plays in a band," Dan added.

"Do his parents know his girlfriend is spending the night?" I wondered.

"Shh…" Chris G. said. "Don't get them in trouble."

It was hard to stop giggling, but we kept quiet because we respected Dave's parents, who were kind to allow four strange adults to sleep in their home and give them giant muffins, and we would have been mortified to meet them.

BROOKLYN AT 3:00 A.M.

As we approached NYC in the Dodge Caravan, I felt giddy. Jasper, Pianos' booker and an amazing photographer, welcomed us as if we were longtime friends. Rob O. and Tom, our friends from UCSB, came to our first show, and Dan and I slept at Rob's railroad apartment in Greenpoint, leaving the next day only to eat pierogis.

The next night, we loaded our gear into a tiny back room at Boogaloo in Brooklyn. Everything had been arranged via email with Mike, the promoter, and I felt very out of my element because our set time wasn't until 3:00 a.m. That never happened in San Francisco.

Groups of people stood on the sidewalk smoking, many women wearing boots over jeans, and I thought to myself, "Please stay. It's just another four hours to our set." To shake some nervous energy, I walked around the corner to Broadway and bought a toothbrush in a convenience store where a cat was giving itself a bath next to the tabloid newspaper rack.

Around 1:00 a.m. Dan, Mai, CW, and I took a cab to Royal Oak, a bar where Christian, our drummer from Secadora, was working. Chris G. was in the van, catching up on sleep because he'd run in the Brooklyn half-marathon that morning. Seeing a longtime friend and former bandmate in a faraway place helped to settle my nerves temporarily. It just felt like this show was going to be weird.

Back at Boogaloo, Mike said, "Time is tight. You'll have about twenty minutes before the party changes the crowd."

We moved our stuff onto the stage as quickly as possible. After the first song in our set, CW stepped away from the drum kit, and I started to play "You Drive," which begins with only my guitar. CW slipped into the bathroom while the crowd watched. After a few minutes, his girlfriend, Mai, knocked on the bathroom door. People danced and stared at us, and the audience was growing, bodies pressing into the small space. I wanted people to come, and now they were here, but would CW ever come out of the bathroom? Dan layered on guitar and Chris G. played bass. We hadn't planned for a drumless set, but if we had to, we'd do that. A security guard got involved. The door opened. CW returned to the stage. People cheered. We played four songs in all and then moved our gear through the sea of bodies to the van as Mike, the promoter, deejayed and the crowd changed into a mob of dancers.

Touring is fun, never boring, but it can be intense. Often the only personal space available is in a bathroom and the only sleep happens in the van. There are times when it's impossible to know how to cope and communicate. Sometimes everything comes apart at the seams in front of an audience. Sometimes it comes back together when strangers are watching too. We never talked with CW about that night because he resurfaced and we pulled off the show. But that didn't mean something like that would never happen again.

ONLY THE CLOTHES ON OUR BACKS

The last show of the US tour was back in Tucson, where I'd had pink eye on the way to SXSW almost two months before. The timing of our return worked to catch some of our favorite bands play Coachella. We parked the minivan in a dusty lot, climbed out, locked it up, and spent the next twelve hours seeing the Rapture, Radiohead, the Pixies, Kraftwerk, and a handful of other bands in the oppressive daytime heat and cool desert night air.

CW left with Mai at the end of the night and Chris G., Dan, and I exited with the masses. Covered in a film of desert sweat, I could not wait to take a shower at Dan's mom's house in Upland and drive home in the morning.

But there was something going on in the parking lot.

"They came through here with a U-Haul and stole everything!" someone shouted.

Glass glittered in the dirt as cars maneuvered past us. Every vehicle in the lot we'd parked in had been broken into, windows smashed. The Dodge Caravan's passenger side window was a large hole, pieces of glass hanging like dew drops from a spiderweb, and the door was open.

"Oh, shit," Chris G. said.

Dan's and my suitcases full of dirty tour clothes were gone. My clamshell iBook was missing, along with my DVD of *Romancing the Stone*.

"All my stuff is still here," Chris G. said.

"Fishy," Dan said, and we laughed.

Nobody could sit in the passenger seat because it was covered in glass. We couldn't close the window because it no longer existed. The next morning, we washed the only clothes we had, while wearing Dan's mom's bathrobes, and finally we drove home.

JOBS BETWEEN TOURS

Dan worked for a commercial real estate start-up, CW worked for pre-IPO Google, and Chris G. worked as an economic analyst. I temped because I couldn't commit to teaching a full semester with more touring on the horizon. We met up at night for band practice and at shows and parties, but during the day we sat at computers.

After the US tour, I pressured myself to apply for and accept a fulltime job as a marketing assistant for a trade magazine. In the office I felt like a caged cat, but I was able to do some band stuff there. Our friends Randy and Lara introduced us to the teen beach drama *The OC*, which Dan and I got hooked on, nostalgic for our beachside life in Santa Barbara. I mailed a CD, a band photo, and a letter to Alexandra Patsavas, the music supervisor for *The OC*, explaining that we were a California band and that our song "Appearances" would be a natural fit on the show. From my cubicle on Second and Harrison Streets in San Francisco I licensed less than a minute of "Appearances" for an episode of the popular FOX show.

Sheetal Singh, who I'd met six years earlier when our bands were playing at the Tip Top Inn, sat in the cubicle next to me. She had a day job as a copyeditor while playing bass in the Stratford 4. We talked about touring and recording, and I didn't feel like I was living a double life as much as I would have without her there, especially on workdays after late shows. To her, I was able to confide my ecstatic emotions when Citizens Here and Abroad's first UK tour was confirmed.

WHITE TRANSIT VAN

The day of our flight to London, Dan and I took BART from MacArthur station to SFO with our guitars and the two small suitcases we'd purchased on sale at Macy's. With CW and Chris G., we landed at Heathrow on a Sunday. After passing through customs, we rolled our luggage carts through a series of tunnels toward Terminal 3 looking for a Dutch guy named Gijs (pronounced "Guy-zhuh") who we were told would deliver a white Ford Transit tour van loaded with amps and a drum kit. Everything had been arranged by Torkel Skogman, a Swedish agent who had booked successful tours for bands we knew. There were options for Terminal 3, though: the car park, arrivals and departures, a ramp going up, stairs going up, and a tunnel ahead.

Dan climbed the stairs and did not find Gijs. CW and I stood by our carts while Dan explored the car park and Chris G. continued forward in the tunnel. We finally found Gijs upstairs, outside the Terminal 3 car park with the van, its back windows taped over with plastic, tape, and a sign in Dutch warning about "asbest."

"Can you translate this for us?" we asked Gijs.

He shrugged. "It says beware, there is asbestos in the van."

"Will it be dangerous to drive around in?" I asked.

"This sign is fiction," Gijs said, "to prevent thieves."

After helping us load our gear into the van Gijs said, "Can you drop me off at Terminal 4 so I can find a bar and watch the World Snooker Championships?"

Chris G. navigated a series of roundabouts. Because the van was Dutch, the steering wheel was on the left, like we were used to, but we were on the left side of the road, which none of us were accustomed to. Before Gijs stepped onto the curb at Terminal 4, he offered two points of advice. One: "The van does not go above 120 kmh." Two: "The least expensive petrol is in Belgium."

We didn't have any shows in Belgium. But we had thirteen shows in the UK and one in Copenhagen. I'd brought along a *London A–Z Map Atlas* and all the road maps AAA offered for the UK. Dan and Chris G. bravely took turns driving. I'd never mastered driving a manual transmission. CW was not allowed to drive on tour anymore since he fell asleep easily.

Our white Dutch Transit van, 2005; Surrey, England

SAXMUNDHAM

Sarah and Ollie, friends we stayed with in London, said, "Saxmundham? Sounds like a made-up place."

The van ran on diesel and the stereo in the cab was missing its face and inoperative, so we spent over two hours on the A12 looking out the window at the greenery. The White Hart, the venue/pub/lodging in Saxmundham, dated from the seventeeth century.

There were flyers for the night's show posted around town, but Citizens Here and Abroad was not listed on them. I spoke with Andrea and Ray Dean, who ran the White Hart. There had been a mix-up. Andrea and Ray Dean added us to the bill and fed us a fish and chips dinner with cans of lukewarm Karlsquell beer. Up a winding staircase, Andrea showed us beds in a cozy attic where we would sleep and a bathroom where none of us could figure out how to operate the shower.

"You're a bit different from the other bands tonight," Andrea said with a shrug.

"We're the only ones from San Francisco?" I said.

"The other bands are still in school," Andrea said.

CW started laughing nervously.

The first group covered Guns N' Roses' "Sweet Child O' Mine" and songs by the Red Hot Chili Peppers. The second band's singer, who doubled as the venue's sound man, had a voice like Tom Waits, unexpected of one so young. The teenage rockers warned us that all the swans in the area belonged to the queen, and we were not to harm them.

"Do you have streams in America?" they asked.

"Yes," we said. "But we call them creeks sometimes."

It was not the best show, and it was not the worst. We were on tour in England. That was enough for me.

VENUE ARCHITECTURE

Playing shows in the UK was like flying first class. UK promoters provided a vegetarian dinner 99 percent of the time, often with fresh bread or rolls and butter and cheese, always with copious cans of room temp beer (forty-eight just for the four of us!). After the last band plays, a DJ comes on and everyone dances like it's the last night on Earth. It's fucking amazing. UK promoters nearly always provided accommodations: two rooms at a Travelodge in Newcastle, soft horse-shaped pillows on a living room floor in Bristol, a bedroom upstairs at an inn. Promoters gave us their spare bedrooms and the morning after ate an English breakfast with us, sometimes with black pudding, sometimes without.

Venues were never in strip malls. Moles was underground, the dinner spread arranged beautifully in a room that resembled a crypt. Upstairs at the Garage in London we unloaded through the back and carried our gear across the main downstairs club, behind the bar, into the kitchen, through a four-foot-tall gap, up three stairs to the landing, up about fifteen more stairs, and into the Upstairs space. I wandered downstairs to the minibar—because there were bars around every corner there, doorways that led to upstairs clubs, attics with teacups in them. In Colchester we played a consecrated church, sound reverberating off the stained-glass windows.

Friends I'd made during my year at the University of Hull—Mike; Shoma; Michaela; Michaela's brother, Chris, and his girlfriend, Maria; Deon; and Matt—came to shows in London, Manchester, and Hull. Our friend Shawn from Little Echoes came to see us in Manchester and Mike shared his home with us. The UK is made for live music. Other bands we played with met back up with us at later shows on the tour.

Backstage at Moles, 2005; Bath, UK

DAYS OFF

We played shows in Colchester and in Leicester and spent a night off in Norwich with my friend Shoma. Members of St. Joan, a band we shared the bill with in London, invited us to Nottingham, where they lived. Not far from famed Sherwood Forest, we ate some questionable Indian take-out and then watched speed dating on TV. One of the speed daters, when asked to describe what he looks for in a woman, said, "She must have teeth."

I woke with a terrible ache in my stomach and feared I'd lose my tikka masala in the bed being loaned to us by a kind young man named George. But I used the power of suggestion to avoid vomiting and told myself that if I did have to hurl, I'd do so into our suitcase, and would not sully George's things.

I felt like I might be able to tour forever, except I was running out of clean underwear. We did laundry at my friend Mike's, but we forgot to use soap, which made our clothes smell worse, so we redid the laundry at Michaela's on our way to Denmark.

OVERNIGHT FERRY

Hull had changed in ten years: supermarkets were now open past 8:00 p.m., and you could find Starbucks and marshmallows. On the way back to Michaela's we drove past the university and my old student accommodation, 76 Cottingham Road. It looked the same.

We parked the van aboard a P&O North Sea Ferry bound for Rotterdam and carried our suitcases to Family Cabin #10343 on deck ten. In the arcade, Chris G. and Dan played *Time Crisis* while I lost control of my rig and crashed repeatedly playing *American Truck Driver*.

Captain Woodhouse announced, "The *Pride of Hull* will only be able to use three of its four engines and therefore we will be delayed forty-five minutes in Rotterdam."

"Do we need four engines?" I asked.

"Hope not," Dan said.

In the ship's disco we watched people move enthusiastically to a mixture of Eurodance music and standard wedding reception tunes. As Michaela forecast, there were many lorry drivers on board. Citizens Here and Abroad were going to Copenhagen for one show on the Continent. Did it make financial sense? No. But it was rock 'n' roll.

COPENHAGEN

Custom officers signaled us to pull over because our front license plate was missing. We received a verbal warning. It was a nine-hour drive to Copenhagen. The cows of Holland and Germany were all lying down.

Andreas the show promoter rode his bicycle to the Copenhagen train station and hopped in the van to direct us to his apartment on Hjort Lorentzensgade. He was eager to talk about bands and music and state taxes and the American forty-hour work week and shoplifting and Guy from Fugazi.

Before we fell asleep in Andreas's living room, an important question was raised.

"Doesn't Andreas look familiar?" Chris G. said.

"He looks like Jon Bon Jovi," Dan said.

"*Slippery When Wet* era Jon Bon," CW said.

We started laughing uncontrollably, as we had in Dave's parents' house in Ohio, but for different reasons.

I wished I'd clipped my fingernails, but it had felt inappropriate in the crowded cabin on the overnight ferry, all four of us plus CW's girlfriend, Mai, sharing one room and bathroom. It felt even more inappropriate in Andreas's apartment.

The next night at the venue, Mai sold an impressive number of CDs and T-shirts. A man came through the club selling flowers and he grabbed at Mai's and my behinds. I punched him in the groin. For the encore we played "The Voices."

The Voices

Take each day one at a time and listen to the voices you
    recognize and weigh each reason for changing your
    mind or doing nothing of the kind.
Jealousy is stronger than wine. Keep drinking.
Awake in the dead of the night planning every day for
    the rest of my life.
I liked you best when you were mine
The weekends, we lost, track of our time.
An excuse became more of a sign, a dead end
Park the car and turn off the lights.
I go. We go. You go. We go.

    —Citizens Here and Abroad, *Ghosts of Tables and Chairs*

HESSLE

A young border agent flagged our Dutch van over at customs upon our return to Hull. "Your front license plate is missing."

I presented our landing card to the agent. He peered into our van. "Who do you know in Hessle?"

"My friend Michaela. From university."

"I also stay in Hessle," the agent said, and he waved us through with a wink.

"Were we just in a Mentos commercial?" Dan said.

We had only three remaining shows: the Adelphi in Hull, the Engine Room in Brighton, and Bitterscene in the Bassment in Chelmsford, outside London. Paul at the Adelphi said he remembered me from the open mic night when Matt and I played years before. The Engine Room in Brighton was a weird, dark venue, a night that ended with sleeping on mattresses on the promoter's kitchen floor. But Bitterscene in Chelmsford was the perfect tour finale.

Paul, one of the promoters, came to the club directly from his train home from work, wearing a suit and tie. We related to him instantly because at home we went straight to shows from work. The other bands on the bill were groups we would have seen even if we weren't playing. Paul and his wife, Jackie, hosted us at their house where we slept on real beds, not on mattresses in a kitchen or pillows in the shape of horses on the floor. Their house was so welcoming, I started to daydream about the new apartment in San Francisco Dan and I would find when we got home. The end of the tour didn't feel so bad.

HOME

After we flew home, Dan and I cat sat for friends Lisa Nola and Adam in Berkeley, waking with felines curled up by our necks. I temped and applied to jobs and Dan went back to his longtime employer. We found an apartment in San Francisco's Mission District with a parking spot. It was walking distance to the Cafe Du Nord, one of our favorite venues.

My house in Fresno smelled of fresh paint when we moved there in 1986 for my mom's new job. Each apartment Dan and I moved into—in 1997, 1998, 2001, 2002, and 2005—had a coat of fresh, white paint. This was our fifth apartment together. The lyrics to "A Change of Scene" from *Ghosts of Tables and Chairs* are about starting all over.

A Change of Scene

Should we change everything, rearrange the furniture, start all over?
It's not too late. It never is. Don't even try to convince me to quit.
The car was packed, the back seat folded down, keep an eye on the highway.

*Don't nod off, promise me you'll stay awake at least
    until I'm ready.*
It looks like you need a change of scene, a change of pace.
I think you'll be all right if we drive through the night.
Everything in its place, the furniture is neatly rearranged
*The carpet's clean, there is no trace of memories the little
    things that stay,*
*through the hours and the days, the furniture its colors
    start to fade*
Ghosts of tables and chairs
*Try to explain everything, I'll memorize, organize my
    life into place*
*It's not too late, it never is, it never was, at least I know
    that much.*

SIGNS OF A PROMISING SHOW

1. Your band's name is on the flyer/poster and the venue is expecting you.

2. The club booker hasn't put you on a metal/reggae/ska/covers/open mic night.

3. It's a club run by a woman or booked by a woman, like Lisa Nola* or Ramona.**

4. The bathroom has toilet paper and toilet seats.

5. There are monitors on the stage and they are in working order during the soundcheck.

6. The soundcheck is not DIY but is conducted by a sound engineer.

7. There is a green room to get nervous/calm down in.

8. You are playing with bands you like.

9. The venue gives you a guest list with plus ones.

10. The audience is enthusiastic.

11. You go home feeling like you want to do this again.

*Lisa Nola ran Eli's Mile High Club in Oakland from August 2004 to August 2005. We performed and went to many shows there during that magical year, often stopping in the bar after band practice.

**At the Bottom of the Hill in San Francisco, Ramona Downey put together some of the best shows, magical billings.

THE GREAT AMERICAN

On August 20, 2005, we played the Great American Music Hall in San Francisco, a favorite venue where I'd seen Animal Collective, Sleater-Kinney, Stereolab, the Decemberists, Modest Mouse, Cat Power, the Shins, my friend Arturo in Slower Than, Blonde Redhead, and dozens of other beloved bands and many years of the Noise Pop Festival. The cooks made us bread pudding, a favorite indulgence since my friend, Caroline, worked at Craig's Bakery in Kailua. Jason showed the "You Drive" video at the start of the set, with Adam controlling the remote. Chris G. and I watched it from behind the screen.

This was the largest venue we'd ever played, two stories tall! Anxiety hit me in the green room and the backstage manager said, loud and clear, "You belong here." We had toured the US and the UK and found our way back home. At the Great American we played what became the first song on our sophomore CD, *Waving, Not Drowning*.

Stranger

I'm not like them. I'm stranger.
It's always the same, same, same conversation and the question,
"Where do we go now?"
And I like you but I'm nervous awkward and apologetic.
It's easy to freak out and fly, fly home.

—Citizens Here and Abroad, *Waving, Not Drowning*

BROTHERS IN SPACE

My youngest brother, Tom, was a freshman at USC when we played Spaceland in LA again on April 10, 2006. He and his friends were under twenty-one, so we ushered them into the club during our load-in, the same as we'd done with my brother Terry when he was at UCLA and underage. My older brother Mark came to the show as well. I was in sixth grade when I learned that I had a brother thirteen years older than me.

To see Mark and Tom in the same audience, my two half brothers, helped to make my family whole. The last time we played Spaceland, Keanu Reeves was in the audience. He's part Chinese like me, Terry, and Mark. The three of us share the same mom. Tom, Terry, and I have the same dad. It was the first time that these two brothers were in the same place at the same time with me.

LAST LEG

We played Pianos in NYC once more in the fall of 2006, on tour for *Waving, Not Drowing*. In photos, Jasper cataloged the era of indie rock music and DIY touring before digital music and smartphones took over. Dan's aunts, uncles, and cousins came from Pennsylvania to see us. Family support is genuine and sincere and especially heartwarming during tour when you're far from home.

From NYC we flew to London for a second UK tour. Our first show was back at Moles in Bath, where we enjoyed fried bread balls for dinner and covered Joy Division's "Disorder." There are stories from that tour, including working out within ten feet of Liam Gallagher at a Marriott gym in London, but nothing is quite like the first time out, when there's nothing to compare it to and there's magic in the air.

Torkel added a show in Birmingham at the last minute, after we'd returned our tour van. Would it be worth it? We decided that we were in the UK to play, so we rented a new van and left London. At the venue, called Scruffy Murphy's, we found out that the included accommodations meant we'd be sleeping on a dorm room floor. Before sunrise we snuck out of the student residence hall and drove to a roadside Starbucks where we sipped hot beverages in silence, all of us sleep-deprived and deflated.

The UK tour ended at Bitterscene again, the best last show in England.

Jet-lagged in San Francisco two days later, I felt like I was floating during our set, watching us play from somewhere in the rafters. The end of a tour is always a sort of out-of-body experience. You know the songs backward and forward. You've memorized the set list like your high school locker combo, able to unlock each song with your eyes closed. Onstage, you can handle everything and off stage, barely anything at all.

Our last show was in LA at El Cid about a week later, in early November. LA shows were always fun; the drive was easy, we stayed with friends, and the Mexican food was the best. But after that tour we all needed a break, some time off, some space.

In four years, we had written and recorded two albums as Citizens Here and Abroad. We'd toured the US in CW's Dodge minivan, played SXSW, and knew which motel chains offered the best free hot breakfast. We'd toured the UK twice. In music I found belonging and purpose, adventure, and people I would have never met otherwise, including my husband. By the end of the second UK tour, however, we couldn't ignore that the seams were starting to come apart. Citizens Here and Abroad disbanded in 2007.

Pianos, October 7, 2006; New York City. Left to Right: Dan Lowrie, Adrienne Robillard, CW, Chris G. Photo by Jasper Coolidge.

WHAT I WISH I KNEW BEFORE TOURING

1. Give up shaving, or wax before the tour. The less body hair, the better for not stinking up your clothes. One exception: longer hair on the head can cover up evidence of not having showered recently.

2. Have Lasik eye surgery to negate the need for contact lenses on tour.

3. Invest in a quality pair of nail clippers. The ones sold at convenience stores aren't great, and tour hangnails are more than annoying.

4. Clothes: layer and spot clean. Pack ample underwear. Throw pairs away and buy new ones as needed.

5. Pack two or three pairs of shoes, no more, no less. You'll think you want to throw one pair away during the tour but keep them. Your feet will get sick of the other pair. Do not take shoes off in the van. Ever. Do not allow others to take them off either.

6. Use the hotel/motel gym. Even twenty minutes on an old treadmill can make you feel so much better after long hours on the road.

7. Eat fresh fruit and vegetables whenever possible to offset all the crap that you will eat and to avoid constipation. That half tomato with the English breakfast? Eat it. That banana in a basket at the 7-Eleven checkout? Buy it.

8. There will be few ideal situations in which to go number two. Time will be a factor. So will cleanliness. You will lower your standards.

9. Pack your own towel, even if it's a hand towel. Anything is better than trying to dry your entire body with a pair of your own jeans.

10. If any booker says "accommodations included," ask for details. If you have any doubt about where you are staying, pay for a hotel or motel. If you need to, blame it on being allergic to dogs/smoke/dust/perfume or on your drummer's sleep screaming. The accommodations may be the promoter's home, and he/she/they/their boyfriend/cousin/sister/uncle will want to party/talk/listen to music all night and you might not want to.

You will be tired.

You will have fun.

You will meet people you'd never have otherwise.

You will be glad you did this.

PLAYLIST

The Smiths, "London"
Sonic Youth, "Dirty Boots"
The Wedding Present, "Dalliance"
Drop Nineteens, "Delaware"
New Order, "Ceremony"
Tears for Fears, "Mad World"
The English Beat, "Save It for Later"
Slowdive, "When the Sun Hits"
The Jesus and Mary Chain, "You Trip Me Up"
The House of Love, "Christine"
Jane's Addiction, "Ocean Size"
Galaxy 500, "Fourth of July"
Cocteau Twins, "For Phoebe Still a Baby"
The Specials, "Too Much Too Young"
Primus, "Jerry Was a Race Car Driver"
Depeche Mode, "Behind the Wheel"
The Cure, "The Blood"
The Fall, "What You Need"
PiL, "Public Image"
Bauhaus, "All We Ever Wanted Was Everything"
The Sugarcubes, "Birthday"

Nirvana, "About a Girl"
Spacemen 3, "I Love You"
The Pet Shop Boys, "Suburbia"
The Replacements, "Anywhere's Better Than Here"
The Red Hot Chili Peppers, "Under the Bridge"
Barbara Manning, "Scissors"
Ride, "Dreams Burn Down"
My Bloody Valentine, "Only Shallow"
Stereolab, "John Cage Bubblegum"
Th' Faith Healers, "Reptile Smile"
PJ Harvey, "Dry"
Chapterhouse, "Pearl"
Melvins, "Going Blind"
Fugazi, "Waiting Room"
Eric's Trip, "Behind the Garage"
Pavement, "In the Mouth a Desert"
Weezer, "The World Has Turned and Left Me Here"
Mudhoney, "Touch Me I'm Sick"
Pixies, "Where Is My Mind?"
Beastie Boys, "Pass the Mic"
Beck, "Sleeping Bag"
The Chemical Brothers, "Life Is Sweet"
Portishead, "Mysterons"
Oasis, "Live Forever"
Blur, "Girls and Boys"
The Breeders, "No Aloha"
Suede, "She's Not Dead"
Pulp, "Common People"
The Verve, "This Is Music"
Soundgarden, "Rusty Cage"
Leftfield, "Space Shanty"

Interpol, "NYC"
Neutral Milk Hotel, "In the Aeroplane Over the Sea"
Belle and Sebastian, "The Boy with the Arab Strap"
Young Marble Giants, "Credit in the Straight World"
Cat Power, "Nude as the News"
Blonde Redhead, "In Particular"
Sleater-Kinney, "Words and Guitar"
The Delgados, "Pull the Wires from the Wall"
Grandaddy, "Broken Household Appliance National Forest"
TV on the Radio, "Staring at the Sun"
The Decemberists, "Billy Liar"
…And You Will Know Us by the Trail of Dead, "Baudelaire"
The White Stripes, "The Hardest Button to Button"
Arcade Fire, "Neighborhood #2 (Laika)"
The Yeah Yeah Yeahs, "Rich"
The Rapture, "I Need Your Love"
The Flaming Lips, "Do You Realize?"
The Postal Service, "The District Sleeps Alone Tonight"
The Shins, "Mine's Not a High Horse"
Radiohead, "Where I End and You Begin"
Modest Mouse, "Bury Me With It"
Bloc Party, "Banquet"
The Thermals, "No Culture Icons"
Broken Social Scene, "Stars and Sons"

CODA

During the pandemic lockdown in the spring of 2020, Dan bought a drum kit and set it up in our converted garage in Kailua, not unlike the kit in my mom's garage in Fresno, where this all started. I still have the bass I bought in Ventura in 1995 to make a new band with him. It feels like time to write music again.

ACKNOWLEDGEMENTS

To Dan, my guy. To our kids, Bea and Ian. To my mom, for buying me my first guitar, driving me to all-ages shows in Fresno and San Francisco, and everything. To my dad and stepmom for letting me see the Red Hot Chili Peppers at Aloha Tower when I was fourteen. Thank you to my cousins, Jeff and Kevin Gin, for my first electric guitar and amp. To my brothers, Terry, Tom, and Mark, for coming to shows, and my sister, Zandra, for years of support. Thanks to Matt and Callie Lowrie, Judy and Mike Florey, and many cousins and aunts and uncles and family for coming to shows over the years, often in unsavory locations that smelled weird.

To my friends in music, starting with Cindy Furey, Craig Sullivan, Jon Eropkin, Kyle Oakes, Arturo Diaz, Thomas from Norway, Debbie Wichmann, Jamie Gluck, Laurel Hitchin, Dianna Jaynes, Jenny Padilla, Mike Leverentz, Ashod Simonian, Isaac Bess, Amaya Aragones-Lopez, Steve Villata, David Harrison, David Horn, Michaela Barnard, Cielo Roth, Eric Schulz, Lisa Nola, Adam Marks, Heather Choy, Chrissy Loader, Sheetal Singh, Mai Le, Jason Koxvold, Jason Smith, Andy Stedman, Susie Meserve, Amy Lewis, Sarah

Brown, Claire Lim and Paul McCallum, Silver Rocket Rachel and Andy, Shawn Biggs, Ramona Downey, Torkel Skogman, Mark Kaiser, Jeff Walsh, Shawn Reynaldo, college stations KFSR, KCSB, JAM, and KALX, all the bookers, Noise Pop and SXSW festivals, and other bands we had the fortune to see and hear.

To all those I've had the fortune of playing music and touring with: Dan Lowrie, Dan Kanzler, Jordan Lambrecht, Shoma Garai, Matt Overson, CT Holman, Rob Ogus, Charles Zuhoski, Brendan Schoen, Christian Serra, Chris Scholz, Kjrsten Haaland, Chris Groves, Chris Wetherell, Jane Pinckard, Film School, Thee More Shallows, Chadwick Bidwell, Tom Marzella, and all the bands and artists that create the soundtracks to our lives. There are too many names to list here, but you know who you are.

Thank you to my friends including Kerri Norman, Richard Lamanna, Holly Watson, Susie Meserve, Susan Blumberg-Kason, Aunt Shirley, Aunt Robin, Uncle Gary, Uncle Victor, Aunt Fran, Tristan Hartmann, Reva Headley, Don Piliero, Arthur Chan, Tess Bevernage, Andria Alefi and Jaime at *We'll Never Have Paris*, Liz Harmer, and my online writing group—Wendra, Gwenyth, and Lindsey. Thanks to Peggy and Keith Zeilinger, whose home was my writing space while they traveled; the Kailua Racquet Club, where I wrote the first draft of this in my car while my daughter played tennis; and Morning Brew in Kailua, one of my favorite places to put words on the page. And thank you to Dawn Sakamoto Paiva and Darien Gee, for your faith and guidance and this opportunity, and the Haliʻa Aloha cohort.

Adrienne Robillard is an English lecturer at Windward Community College. She grew up in Kailua, Hawai'i, and Fresno, California. After college she worked in San Francisco as an office temp and marketing professional by day, playing in indie bands at night. She lives with her husband and their two children in Kailua on O'ahu. In 2020 her first book of barbecue, *The 'Ohana Grill Cookbook*, was published by Ulysses Press.

www.adriennerobillard.com

www.ingramcontent.com/pod-product-compliance
Lightning Source LLC
Chambersburg PA
CBHW072040110526
44592CB00012B/1497